Teach Yourself
to Play
Chord Piano/Keyboard
At Home Without a Teacher

Teach Yourself
to Play
Chord Piano/Keyboard
At Home Without a Teacher

Taylor Learning Resource Center Inc.

To order additional copies of this book, contact:
Xlibris Corporation
1-888-795-4274
www.Xlibris.com
Orders@Xlibris.com
51108

CONTENTS

INTRODUCTION

Taylor Learning Resource Center Inc., following more than twenty-eight years of teaching children and adult music lessons, has decided to publish a home study course: *Teach Yourself to Play Chord Piano/Keyboard at Home Without a Teacher!* Taylor Learning Resource Center Inc. has successfully taught thousands of people to play the piano, keyboard, and organ by chording. In this book, the three primary chords for the keys of C, F, and G will be introduced. The student will also learn how to play the primary chords in rhythmic form along with the melody line.

This course is user-friendly for the young learners, older beginners, and experienced individuals who would like to learn how to chord. The book is specifically designed for those who do not have the time and/or finance for music lessons, which can be expensive. This course is a great resource for those who desire to teach themselves, children, or grandchildren in the comfort of their home.

MUSICAL ALPHABET

The musical alphabet is:

A   B   C   D   E   F   G

The musical alphabet keeps repeating itself.

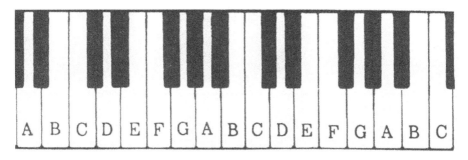

The colors of the keys on the piano keyboard are black and white.

The black keys are arranged in patterns of 2's and 3's.

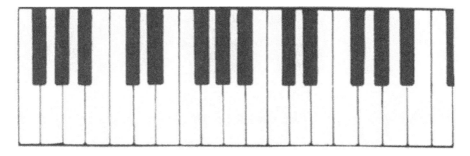

LOCATION OF KEYS

In order to play the piano, you need to know where the keys are located.

The black keys on the piano keyboard can be used as a guide to locate the keys.

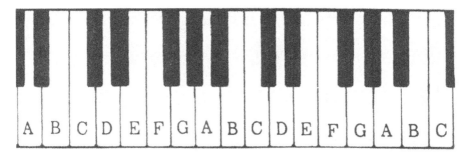

A   is located between the second and third keys of the group of three black keys.

B   is located to the right of the group of three black keys.

C   is located to the left of the group of two black keys.

D   is located between the groups of two black keys.

E   is located to the right of two black keys.

F   is located to the left of three black keys.

G   is located between the first and second keys of the group of three black keys.

IDENTIFYING THE KEYS

Write in all the C's, B's, and F's on the keyboard.

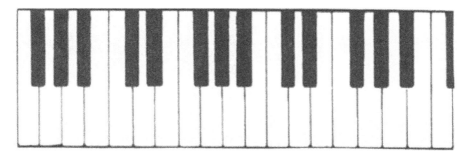

Write in all the D's, G's, and A's on the keyboard.

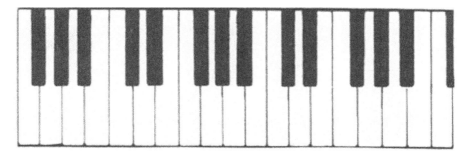

Write in all the E's, G's, B's, C's and D's on the keyboard.

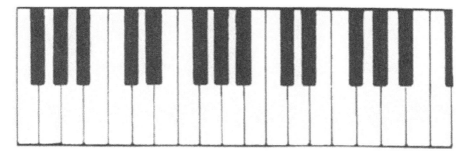

PLAYING THE KEYS

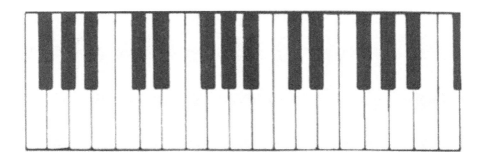

Play all the A's on the keyboard.

Play all the B's on the keyboard.

Play all the C's on the keyboard.

Play all the D's on the keyboard.

Play all the E's on the keyboard.

Play all the F's on the keyboard.

Play all the G's on the keyboard.

Continue playing the notes over and over until mastery is achieved.

NAMING THE KEYS

Write the names of the keys on the dashes.

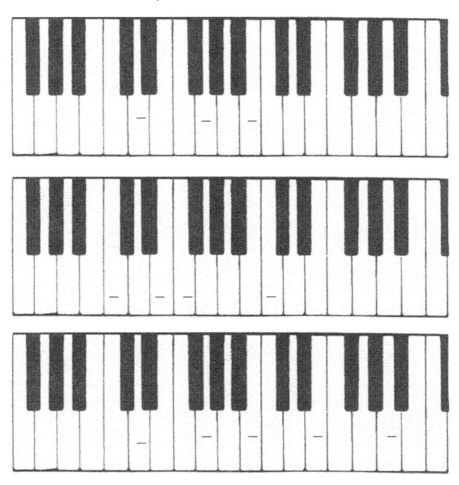

You are ready to play **Come by Here** in the key of C with your right hand.

Positioning:

1. Face forward and find the center of the keyboard.
2. The first C to your left is the middle C.

COME BY HERE

C C E G G   A A G

Come by here my Lord. Come by here.

C C E G G   E E D

Come by here my Lord. Come by here.

C   C E G G   A A G

Come by here my Lord. Come by here.

F EC D   D   C

Oh Lord come by here.

Play repeatedly until you master the song.

KEY OF C

In this session, you will learn three primary chords in the key of C.

The primary chords are: C F G7.

C Chord

Whenever you play a C, E, or G in the melody with your right hand, play the C chord with your left hand.

The C chord is C, E, G.

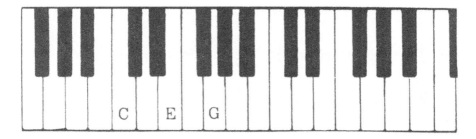

Play the C, E, and G all at the same time.

Continue playing the C chord over and over until you master the chord.

F CHORD

Whenever you play an F or A in the melody with your right hand, play the F chord with your left hand at the same time.

The F chord is F, A, C.

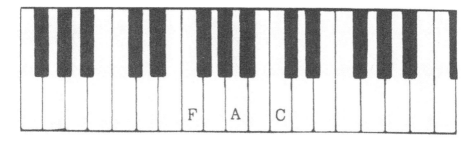

Play the F, A, and C all at the same time.

Continue playing the F chord over and over until you master the chord.

G7 Chord

Whenever you play D or B in the melody with your right hand, play the G7 chord with your left hand.

The G7 chord is F, G, B.

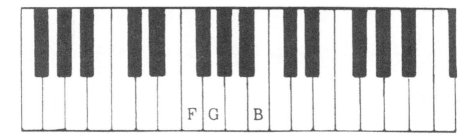

Play F, G, and B all at the same time.

Keep playing the G7 chord over and over until you master the chord.

Play the C, F, G7 chord over and over again until you master the chords.

CHORDING THE C MAJOR SCALE

The C major scale is: C, D, E, F, G, A, B, C.

Play C with your right hand, along with the C chord with your left hand.

Play D with your right hand, along with the G7 chord with your left hand.

Play E with your right hand, along with the C chord with your left hand.

Play F with your right hand, along with the F chord with your left hand.

Play G with your right hand, along with the C chord with your left hand.

Play A with your right hand, along with the F chord with your left hand.

Play B with your right hand, along with the G7 chord with your left hand.

Play C with your right hand, along with the C chord with your left hand.

Continue chording the C major scale over and over until mastery is achieved. Now we will play **Come by Here** with both hands. The right hand will play the melody and the left hand will play the chords.

Key of C

COME BY HERE

C   C E G G   A A G

Come by here my Lord. Come by here.

C   C E G G   E E D

Come by here my Lord. Come by here.

C   C E G G   A A G

Come by here my Lord. Come by here.

F EC D D C

Oh Lord come by here.

*   *   *

C Chord is CEG played with C, E, or G.

F Chord is FAC played with F or A.

G7 Chord is FGB played with D or B.

Key of C

O HOW I LOVE JESUS

E E D E   CC   D D C D   EGG

O how I love Jesus.   O how I love Jesus.

E E D E   CC   EDE   F   E D   C

O   how I love Jesus. Because He first loved me.

C   E E ED E C   C C

There is a name I love to hear.

C D   D DC D   EG

I love to sing its worth,

C   E   E   DED C C   C

It sounds like music to mine ear.

E   DEF   E   D C

The sweetest name on earth.

Key of C

OCTAVE

An octave means to play eight scale notes higher or lower.

Example:

A to A is an octave.

B to B is an octave.

E to E is an octave.

G to G is an octave.

˙L means to play the lower letter note to your left.

˙h means to play the higher letter note to your right.

Key of C

HOLY, HOLY, HOLY

CC   EE   GG   A   A   A G E
Holy Holy Holy Lord God Almighty

G G G G *hC B
Early in the morning,

G   D   G   A G G
Our song shall rise to thee.

CC   EE   GG   A A A A   G E
Holy Holy Holy merciful and mighty,

*hC G   G   AE   F D D C C
God in three persons blessed trinity.

*h stands for high. This means an octave higher.

Key of C

NOTHING BUT THE BLOOD OF JESUS

C   C   D   CE   G   E

What can wash away my sins?

C   C   C   D   E   E   DC

Nothing but the blood of Jesus.

C   C   D   C   E   GE

What can make me whole again?

CC   C   D   E   E   DC

Nothing but the blood of Jesus.

G   EC   E   G   E   D   D   C

O precious is the flow that makes me

E   G   E   G   EC   E   G   E

white as snow. No other fount I know

C   C   C   D   E   E   DC

nothing but the blood of Jesus.

Key of C

24

COME TO JESUS

C   C   C^{L}G   E   E   EC

Come to Jesus come to Jesus.

E   E   GF   E   D

Come to Jesus just now.

DE   F   GF EDC

Just now just now.

C   E   DC ^{L}B   C

Come to Jesus just now.

*L stands for low. This means an octave lower.

Key of C

My Faith Looks Up to Thee

C   E   G G F E

My faith looks up to Thee,

D   D   F F E D

Thou lamb of Cal-va-ry,

E   D A G

Sav-iour di-vine,

G E F G A G

Now hear me while I pray,

G E F G AG

take all my guilt away.

*hC B A G F

O let me from this

E C D G C

day be whol-ly thine !

*h stands for high. This means an octave higher.

Key of C

WHAT A MIGHTY GOD WE SERVE

G   G G G   G   A GFE

What a mighty God we serve.

G G GG   G   F EDED

What a mighty God we serve.

G G   G   FE   C

Angels bow before Him.

GG   G   G   FE   C

Heaven and earth adore Him.

G   G GF   E   D   C

What a mighty God we serve.

Key of C

Sweet Hour of Prayer

C E F G   G A B *hC

Sweet hour of prayer, sweet hour of prayer,

A G E ED C D E D

That calls me from a world of care

C E F G G A B   *hC

and bid me of my fa-ther's throne.

A G E ED C E D C

Make all my wants and wish-es known

G *hC B *hC AG   E   G

In sea-sons of distress and grief

G *hC B *hCA G   E D

my soul has of-ten found re-lief

C E F G   G A   B *hC

and often es-caped the tempt-er's snare

A G E ED   C   E D C

by thy re-turn, sweet hour of prayer.

*h stands for high. This means an octave higher.

Key of C

HAVE THINE OWN WAY, LORD

E   D   E   F   E   C   *LB   C   D

Have thine own way, Lord! Have thine own way!

D   C   D   ED   DC *LB C

Thou art the Potter; I am the clay.

E   D   E   F   E   GF G A

Mould me and make me after thy will,

A   BA GE   DC   D   C

While I am waiting, yielded and still.

*L stands for low. This means an octave lower.

Key of C

HE GOT THE WHOLE WORLD IN HIS HANDS

G   G   E   G   EC
He's got the whole world—

G   A   G
in His hands,

G   G   E   F   D*LB
He's got the whole world—

G   A   G
in His hands,

G   G   E   G   EC
He's got the whole world—

G   A   G
in His hands,

E   E   F   G   G
He's got the whole world—

F   D   C
in His hands.

*L stands for low. This means an octave lower.

Key of C

I Surrender All

E E FE D DED C C F

All to Jesus I surrender all to Him.

E DE C E E FE D

I freely give. I will ever love

D E D C C FE

and trust Him. In His presence

DE C *hC BAG F

daily live. I surrender all,

B AGF E

I surrender all.

E F A G *hC B BA

All to thee, my blessed Savior

G FED C

I surrender all.

*h stands for high. This means an octave higher.

Key of C

REACH OUT AND TOUCH

C D E F F E D C

Reach out and touch somebody's hand.

C D E E DC C C D

Make this world a better place if you

C

can.

Key of C

SILENT NIGHT

GA G E GAG E

Si-lent night, ho-ly night.

*hD*hD B *hC*hC G

All is calm, all is bright.

A   A *hCBA   G A

Round young vir-gin, moth-er

G E   A A

and child. Ho-ly

*hC B A G A

in-fant so ten-der

G   E

and mild.

*hD *hD *hF *hD B*hC *hE

Sleep in heav-en-ly peace—.

*hC GE G F D   C

Sleep—in heav-en-ly peace—.

*h stands for high. This means an octave higher.

Key of C

Yes Jesus Loves Me

G EG   A   *hC

Yes Jesus loves me.

G   EC   E   D

Yes Jesus loves me.

G EG   A *hC A A GC

Yes Jesus loves me for the bible

E   D C

tells me so.

GE   E   D   E G G   A

Jesus loves me this I know for

A *hCA A G G

the bible tells me so.

GE   E   D E   GG

Little ones to him belong,

A   A G   C E D C

they are weak but he is strong.

*h stands for high. This means an octave higher.

Key of C

I HAVE DECIDED TO FOLLOW JESUS

C C   EGG G   AG   EC

I have decided to follow Jesus.

*hC*hC*hC*hC*hC*hC*hC D*hC   AG

I have decided to follow Jesus.

C C   EGG G   AG   EC

I have decided to follow Jesus.

G   AG   E   E   DD   C

No turning back, no turning back.

*h stands for high. This means an octave higher.

Key of C

JOY TO THE WORLD

---

*hC B A   G   F   E   D   C

Joy to the world the Lord has come

G   A   AB   B   *hC

let Earth receive her King.

*hC*hCBAG GFE*hC*hCB AG GFE

Let every heart prepare Him room

E   E   E   EEF G

and heaven and nature sing

F   DD   D DDE   F

and heaven and nature sing

ED C*hC   A   GFE   F   E D   C

and heaven and heaven and nature sing.

*h stands for high. This means an octave higher.

Key of C

GLORY BE TO GOD ON HIGH

C   E   G E   GAG   EGAG

Christ was born in Bethlehem alleluia

E G G   E   F   E   D   CDED

son of God and son of man alleluia.

Key of C

THERE IS A FOUNDATION

C E G A G *hC *hC

There is a fountain filled

A   G   C E   G   G A G E   DED

with blood drawn from Immanuel's veins,

CE G A   G   *hC*hC

and sinners plunged beneath

A   G *hC*hD*hE *hC *hD *hE *hC

that flood lose all their guilty stains;

*hC*hD *hE *hC *hD*hE *hCA*hC

loose all their guilty stains,

A G G AG E DED

loose all their guilty stains;

CE G A   G   *hC*hC

and sinners plunged beneath

A   G *hCDE *hC DE *hC

that flood lose all their guilty stains.

*h stands for high. This means an octave higher.

Key of C

BATTLE HYMN OF THE REPUBLIC

G   G   G   G   F   EG *hC *hD *hE*hE *hE *hD *hC

Mine eyes have seen the glory of the coming of the Lord;

*hC *hB A A   A B *hCB   *hC

He is trampling out of vintage where

A   G   A   G   E   G   G   G

the grapes of wrath are stored; He hath

G   G   GF   E G   *hC*hD*hE*hE *hE *hD   *hC

loosed the fateful lightning of his terrible swift sword;

*hC *hC *hD *hC*hB   *hC GGF   EG   *hC*hD*hE*hC

His truth is marching on. Glory! Glory! Hallelujah!

AAB *hCB   *hC A G *hE

Glory! Glory! Hallelujah!

GGF   EG   *hC *hD *hE *hC

Glory! Glory! Hallelujah!

*hC *hD *hD *hC B   *hC

His truth is marching on.

*h stands for high. This means an octave higher.

Key of C

39

WE SHALL OVERCOME

G   G   AA GFE

We shall over come

G   G   AA GFE

We shall over come

G   G   AB *hC*hDBABAC

We shall over come someday

AB*hCB A   G   A   G   FE

Oh, If in our hearts we do believe

G   G   CF E   DC

We shall over come someday

*h stands for high. This means an octave higher

Key of C

SHARP ♯

A sharp raises a note a half step. When a sharp sign is placed before a note, play the very next key to the right.

E♯ is played on the same white key as F.

B♯ is played on the same white key as C.

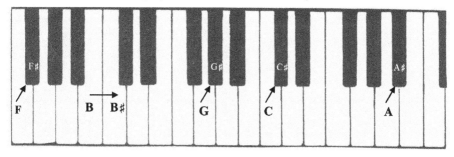

Play all the F♯'s on the keyboard.

Play all the B♯'s on the keyboard.

Play all the G♯'s on the keyboard.

Play all the C♯'s on the keyboard.

Play all the A♯'s on the keyboard.

Continue to play the notes over and over until mastery is achieved.

FLAT ♭

A flat lowers a note a half step. When a flat sign is placed before a note, play the very next key to the left.

C♭ is played on the same white key as B.

F♭ is played on the same white key as E.

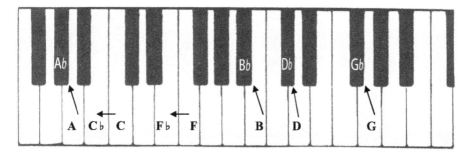

Play all the A♭'s on the keyboard.

Play all the C♭'s on the keyboard.

Play all the F♭'s on the keyboard.

Play all the B♭'s on the keyboard.

Play all the D♭'s on the keyboard.

Play all the G♭'s on the keyboard.

Continue to play the notes over and over until mastery is achieved.

KEY OF F

In this session, you will learn three primary chords in the key of F.

The primary chords are: F   Bb   C7.

F Chord

Whenever you play a F, A, or C in the melody with your right hand, play the F chord with your left hand.

The F chord is F, A, C.

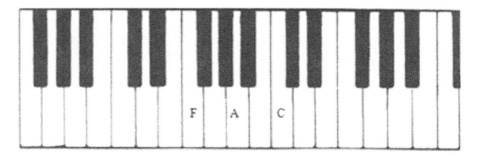

Play the F, A, and C all at the same time.

Continue playing the F chord over and over until you master the chord.

B♭ Chord

Whenever you play a B♭ or D in the melody with your right hand, play the B♭ chord with your left hand at the same time.

The B♭ chord is B♭, D, F.

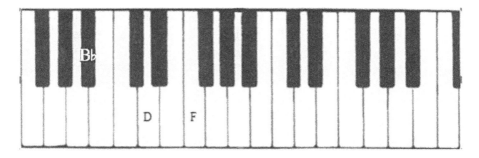

Play the B♭, D, and F all at the same time.

Continue playing the B♭ chord over and over until you master the chord.

C7 CHORD

Whenever you play a C, E, or B♭ in the melody with your right hand, play the C7 chord with your left hand at the same time.

The C7 chord is C, E, B♭.

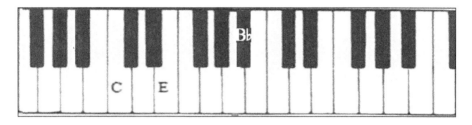

Play the C, E, and B♭ all at the same time.

Continue playing the F, B♭, and C7 chords over and over until you master the chords.

CHORDING THE F MAJOR SCALE

The F major scale is: F, G, A, B♭, C, D, E, F.

Play F with your right hand, along with the F chord with your left hand.

Play G with your right hand, along with the G7 chord with your left hand.

Play A with your right hand, along with the F chord with your left hand.

Play B♭ with your right hand, along with the B♭ chord with your left hand.

Play C with your right hand, along with the F chord with your left hand.

Play D with your right hand, along with the B♭ chord with your left hand.

Play E with your right hand, along with the C7 chord with your left hand.

Play F with your right hand, along with the F chord with your left hand.

Continue chording the F major scale over and over until mastery is achieved. Key of F

COME BY HERE

F   F   A   C   C   D   D   C
Come by here my Lord. Come by here.

F   F   A   C   C   A   A   G
Come by here my Lord. Come by here.

F   F   A   C   C   D   D   C
Come by here my Lord. Come by here.

Bb AF G   G   F
Oh Lord come by here.

*   *   *

F Chord is F, A, C played with F, A, or C.

Bb Chord is Bb, D, F played with Bb or D.

C7 Chord is C, E, Bb played with E or G.

Key of F

No, Not One

A   AG F   G   F

There's not a friend like the

*LD F *LD*LC A A G AG F

lowly Jesus. No not one, no not one

A   A   G   F   G   F

None else could heal all our

*LD F *LD*LC A A G A G F

soul diseases. No not one, no not one

CC C   D CA A   G F

Jesus knows all about our struggles

C   C   C   C D C

He will guide us till the

A A   G

day is done.

A AG F   G   F *LD F *LD*LC

There not a friend like the lowly Jesus.

A A G A G F

No not one, no not one.

*L stands for low. This means an octave lower.

Key of F

AWAY IN A MANGER

C   C   Bb A   A   G

A-way in a manger,

F   F *LE *LD *LC *LC

no crib for His bed, the

*LC D *LC *LC G

lit-tle Lord Je-sus

*LE   *LD *LC   F   A

laid down His sweet head;

C   C   Bb A   AG

The stars in the sky

F   F *LE *LD

looked down where he

*LC *LC Bb A

lay, the lit-tle

G   A G   F   G

Lord Je-sus, a sleep

*LD *LE   F

on the hay.

*L stands for low. This means an octave lower.

Key of F

Blest Be the Ties

A   AF   A G *LE

Blest be—the ties—

G   F   F F*LD

that binds, our hearts—

F   F*LC F *LE

in Christian love

G G*LE G FA C C G Bb

the fel-low-ship of kindred

A C   D CA Bb AF

minds—is like to that

G F

above.

*L stands for low. This means an octave lower.

Key of F

STEAL AWAY

F   F F   A A A

Steal a-way, steal a-way,

C   C   C D G A

steal a-way to Jesus.

F F F   D D

Steal a-way, oh, steal

C A   C   F   F

a-way home, I don't

F   A A G   F

have time to stay here.

Key of F

KEY OF G

In this session, you will learn three primary chords in the key of G.

The primary chords are: G   C   D7.

G Chord

Whenever you play a G, B, or D in the melody with your right hand, play the G chord with your left hand.

The G chord is G, B, D.

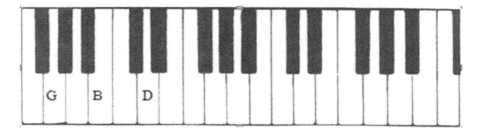

Play the G, B, and D all at the same time.

Continue playing the G chord over and over until you master the chord.

C CHORD

Whenever you play a C or E in the melody with your right hand, play the C chord with your left hand at the same time.

The C chord is C, E, G

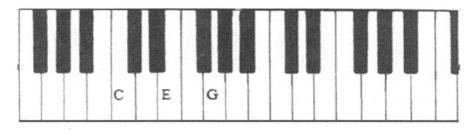

Play the C, E, and G all at the same time.

Continue playing the C chord over and over until you master the chord.

D7 CHORD

Whenever you play A or F♯ in the melody with your right hand, play the D7 chord with your left hand at the same time.

The D7 chord is D, F♯, C.

Play the D, F♯, and C all at the same time.

Continue playing the G, C, and D7 chords over and over until you master the chords.

CHORDING THE
G MAJOR SCALE

The G major scale is: G, A, B, C, D, E, F♯, and G.

Play the G with your right hand, along with the G chord with your left hand.

Play the A with your right hand, along with the D7 chord with your left hand.

Play the B with your right hand, along with the G chord with your left hand.

Play the C with your right hand, along with the C chord with your left hand.

Play the D with your right hand, along with the G chord with your left hand.

Play the E with your right hand, along with the C chord with your left hand.

Play the F♯ with your right hand, along with the D7 chord with your left hand.

Play the G with your right hand, along with the G chord with your left hand.

Continue chording the G major scale over and over until mastery is achieved.

Key of G

Amazing Grace

---

^{*L}D   G   BG   B   A   G

A-maz-ing—Grace! How sweet

*LE *LD *LD   G   BG B   A *hD

the sound, that saved a—wretch like me!—

B *hD B *hD   G   *LD *LE G G*LE

I once—was—lost, but now—am—

*LD *LD   G   BG   B A G

found, was blind, but now I see,—

*   *   *

G Chord is G, B, D played with G, B, or D.

C Chord is C, E, G played with C or E.

D7 Chord is D, F♯, A played with F♯ or A.

*h stands for high. This means an octave higher.

*L stands for low. This means an octave lower.

Key of G

NOBODY KNOWS THE TROUBLE I'VE SEEN

B ^{L}D ^{L}E G   A BB B   B

No bod-y knows the trouble I've seen,

B ^{L}D E   G   G ^{L}E^{L}D

no-bod-y knows but Je-sus.

B ^{L}D ^{L}E G   A BB   B   B

No-bod-y knows the trouble I've seen,

D B A B G G

glo-ry ha-le-lu-jah!

B   D   D

Some-times I'm up,

B   D   D   B

some-times I'm down,

D B   A

oh yes, Lord.

B   D   D D B D D   B

some-times I'm al-most to the ground

B A G

oh yes, Lord.

*L stands for low. This means an octave lower.

Key of G

59

NEARER, MY GOD, TO THEE

B   A   G   G   *LE   *LE
Near-er, my God, to Thee,

*LD   G   B   A
near-er to Thee.

B   A   GG *LE *LE
E'en though it be a cross

*LD G F♯A G
that—raiseth me

D   E   D   D   B   D
still all my song shall be

D   E   D   D   B   A
near-er, my God to Thee

B   A   G   G *LE *LE
near-er, my God to Thee

*LD G F♯ A G
near-er to Thee.

*L stands for low. This means an octave lower.

Key of G

JESUS, KEEP ME NEAR THE CROSS

B C   B A G *LE *LE

Je-sus, keep me near the cross;

*LD G G B   B A

There a pre-cious foun-tain

B C B A G *LE *LE

free to all, a healing stream,

*LD G G *LF♯ A G

flow from Cal-vary's moun-tain,

B D D C E E

In the cross, in the cross

D E D B B A

Be my glo-ry ev-er,

B C B A G

Till my rap-tured soul

*LE *LE *LD G G *LF♯ A G

Shall find rest be-yond the river.

*L stands for low. This means an octave lower.

Key of G

61

O Come, All Ye Faithful

G   G   *LD G   A   *LD
O—come, all ye faith-ful,

B   A   B   C   B   A
Joy—ful and tri-um-phant,

G   G   F♯ E   F♯G   A B   F♯E *LD *LD
O come—ye, O come—ye to Beth-le-hem;

D   C B   C   B
Come—and be—hold Him,

A   B   G   A   F♯ E *LD
Born the king of an—gels;

G   G   F♯G A   G   *LD
O come, let us a-dore Him,

B   B   A B C   B   A
O come, let us a-dore Him

B   C   B A G   F♯
O come, let us a-dore

G C   B A   G   G
Him,—Christ,—the Lord!—

DON'T KNOW WHAT TO TEACH YOUR KIDS? WORRY NO MORE, FOR A BASIC ACADEMIC SKILLS TRAINING GUIDE IS NOW HERE TO HELP YOU!

Taylor Learning Resource Center Inc. Teaches Parents the Importance of Pre-school Education

New book provides basic academic skills training for kids in pre-school

Education is one of the pillars of a progressive society. It is through education that people get jobs to put food on their table. It is also how people earn their degrees, titles, and become renowned experts in different fields, gaining respect and trust from people all around them. An educated constituency, therefore, shapes a nation. Yet people will never reach such a high stage of development if they don't go through the basics. Readers will learn the value of basic education through *Mommy, I Can . . .* , an educational material prepared by the Taylor Learning Resource Center Inc.

Intended to teach kids the basic reading, linguistic, and mathematical skills, *Mommy, I Can . . .* aims to develop their skills and prepares them for an early education. This research-based educational guide allows parents to participate in their kids' academic advancement training. Highly recommended to mothers and teachers alike, it include an array of exercises and tests which boosts children's self-esteem, increases their eagerness to learn, and improves their scholastic performance. From name writing to word analysis, this material proves the significance of early education in every person's developmental stage, for this serves as the foundation for future educational endeavors.

Children go to pre-school only once. It is then necessary that his guardians and teachers provide him with the best tools to aid his education and to propel his mental and emotional maturity. Taylor Learning Resource Center invites parents to show their kids the fun way to learn by giving them *Mommy, I Can . . .*

Mommy, I Can . . . is enrolled in Xlibris' Bookstore Returnability Program, which gives booksellers the convenient option of returning excess stocks through Ingram Distribution. For more information, log on to *www.Xlibris.com*.

*Mommy, I Can * by Taylor Learning Resource Center Inc.*

ORDER A COPY NOW!!!

At Amazon.com, Borders.com, Barnesandnoble.com, or *www.mommyican.net*